MW01141404

Five Elements of Hatha Yoga

A Beginners Handbook

Five Elements of Hatha Yoga

A Beginners Handbook

Karen Watson

KARANA

KARANA

Five Elements of Hatha Yoga
A Beginners Handbook
© 2023 Karen Watson
All rights reserved
London

No part of this publication may reproduced, stored in a
retrieval system or transmitted in any form or by any means
graphic, electronic, mechanical including photocopying,
recording or by any other means without prior written
permission from the author

Cover and chapters artworks © Dominika Klimczak
Chapters diagrams © Chathuri Sugandhika
Portrait photography © Kush Rattan

Edited by John Evans

Set in Libre Baskerville
Typeset by Eva Megias
Printed and bound in Great Britain by
Short Run Press.

British Library Cataloguing-in-Publication Data
Karen Watson
ISBN 978-1-3999-4910-1

The author shall not accept any liability or responsibility
to any person or entity with regards to any injury, damage
or loss caused or alleged to be caused directly or indirectly
from the information in this book. This book and the
information contained within it is in no way intended to be
used as a substitute for a teacher. The advice of a health care
professional should be sought before attempting any of the
movements or practices described herein

Table of Contents

Acknowledgements

I give thanks to my teacher Sundernath (Shándor Remete) for his guidance over three decades and whose ceaseless personal inquiry has been a beacon of light on the path of yoga.

A genuine teacher-student relationship is a rare blessing in our modern world.

To Emma Balnaves for her talent and commitment in bringing the teachings of Shadow Yoga to a wider audience and for her support and friendship in both teaching and learning.

To my husband and soulmate John Evans for his support and encouragement on the journey.

And to all the students through whom I learnt the most about teaching what is in this book.

It would not have been possible without the contribution of all these people.

Foreword

The body and speech are of
the nature of courage and particle;
while the mind is of the nature of darkness
and so the origin of the difficulty that one encounters
upon the path of self-cultivation.

It is austerity that possesses the power
to take one beyond this obstacle,
since it rids the individual not only of grief but also of joy,
employing the barest minimum of means or equipment.

There are two types of people upon this path.
The first is the one who is in constant upheaval
in order to gain mastery.
The other is the one who is gathered
and is beyond doubt and its wickedness.

The author of this book is one of these.
She gives the early steps of how to proceed
with reversing the outward flowing of life.
The art and craft of hatha yoga, once attained,
reaches its final act referred to as jataveda - sacrificial fire
- that part of fire that delivers the offering into the fire.
It is called antyeṣṭi - the last sacrifice or rite.
This takes place within the hue of the natural state,
where one strolls upon the pathway of reality.

Therefore, this fire is the last rite of passage
which returns the body to its origins
earth - water - fire - air - space
and finally the great void of light that is beyond all,
the domain of eternal life.

Hence the hidden meaning in the title of the book.
One must reflect deeply and tread with caution
so as not to break the thread that is used
to weave the cloak of self-illumined freedom.
So be it!

Sundernath (Shandor Remete)

Introduction

There has been an explosion of interest in yoga in the west over the last three decades and a huge variety of classes and other forms of instruction are available. Many of those who are interested begin classes which are physically demanding while others will be drawn to more gentle yoga practices which focus on relaxation or methods of meditation. The more physically oriented yoga classes range from the practice of sequences of dynamic physical movements to those where positions are held for extended periods of time, with or without a conscious focus on the breathing. Classes that focus on relaxation or meditation may or may not include many physical postures but concentrate on different breathing exercises and techniques to calm the nervous system. It is rare to find a class that approaches all aspects of the body, breath and mind in a balanced way.

In the ancient hatha yoga texts, it is clearly assumed there is already some proficiency in being able to sit comfortably in a crossed legged or other meditative position, often the lotus posture (*padmāsana*), and maintain concentration for extended periods of time. Arriving at this point clearly involves some preliminary training but there is little information on what that might be. It is difficult to know how different the culture and lifestyles of those practicing yoga then was compared to the situation of those who begin learning yoga today and thus what kind of preparatory work would have been required. Some suggest that the lack of information available is because yoga was taught on an individual basis by a teacher who would observe the capabilities of the student and guide them accordingly. The yoga texts are full of metaphorical terms that can only make sense with a practical understanding of the activity. This understanding would be imparted through instruction from the teacher, verbally or non-verbally. Such transmission took place when the student was ready and the teacher-student relationship was held in high regard. It is easy to go astray if the meaning behind specific terms is misunderstood. This is still true nowadays, even more so due to the incomplete knowledge of the culture surrounding the practice of yoga at the time the texts were written. Thus the importance of a teacher or guide cannot be overstated. One is needed to ensure the practice is done correctly to avoid injuries and problems that may arise from not knowing what or how much to do. Human beings are also creatures of habit and tend to gravitate towards things they like to do and avoid the things they don't like. The teacher is also there to provide discipline in this direction. Sometimes things need to be done that are not particularly to one's liking or preferences. It can be hard to recognise this and follow through on one's own.

What is apparent in the yoga texts is that all three aspects, the body, breath, and mind are involved in the practice. The bodily or physical activity is necessary to cultivate a stable seated posture for the internal breathing and meditative practices. Such a posture also needs to be free from obstructions or restrictions that impede the flow of energy in the body. However, being able to sit in the correct posture is in itself not enough. It is also necessary to be able to maintain the focus of the mind on the breathing and the movement of the breath in the body. This is a finely balanced skill which is neither falling asleep or daydreaming nor obsessively focussing or fixing the mind on a single point. It is a focus that is both alert and responsive, being able to observe when the mind wanders off into daydreaming or otherwise and being able to guide the attention back to where it needs to be. It is a particular focus that can be cultivated from the very beginning of learning yoga and that has as much to do with the body as the mind.

This book presents a series of yoga practices that will take one in this direction both physically and mentally. As one undertakes the different practices there will be changes in the physical shape of the body as the body becomes stronger and more flexible. There will also be physiological changes in processes such as digestion, circulation and breathing as well as in the way one relates to them. The principles that are used in yoga to describe these processes have as their basis the concept of the five elements that evolved within ancient Indo-European culture. The elements are arranged in the sequence of earth, water, fire, air and space. This sequence is one of increasing subtlety with earth as the most gross element and space, or ether, the most refined. They are understood to relate to the different parts of the body as well as influence different bodily functions. This provides a map for connecting with the natural intelligence within that is ultimately responsible for health and healing.

With this in mind I have used the five elements to convey the progressive nature of the yoga practices from gross to subtle. Together these practices provide the tools to begin the process of integrating the body, mind and breath and make steady improvements in physical health and mental well-being. This integration is key to learning the Shadow Yoga preludes. These preludes were conceived by Sundernath (Shandor Remete), the founder of Shadow Yoga, as a way to cultivate the prerequisites for the practices described in the hatha yoga texts.

What is presented in this book is the outcome of teaching Shadow Yoga to all levels of students over the past twenty five years. It is intended as a resource for complete beginners of yoga. It may also benefit those who have some experience of yoga but who sense something missing in the connection between the body, breath and mind. It is for those who seek a clear direction in the practice of hatha yoga.

Earth

Stances

Foundation

Earth: Foundation

Any endeavour requires a sound foundation if it is to yield success. This is also true in yoga. In this first chapter we deal with the preliminary joint warm up sequence or *caraṇas* and the standing movements that provide this foundation.

Caraṇas

Joint warm ups are very common in many physical disciplines as well as in a number of yoga systems but are largely absent in many schools of mainstream yoga. One text, the *Hatha Tattva Kaumudi* outlines a daily practice for the beginner where the repetitions of the *caraṇas* are steady built up to 50 times over a period of time and then maintained at this level for a few months.

The following is a sequence of *caraṇas* that release tension in the body through a step-by-step process.

Ankles - feet behind, rotating outwards first then inwards
Head and neck.

1) turning side to side.

2) bending side to side.

3) forward and back.

Shoulders – rolling forward and back.

Wrist movements - elbows close keeping the hands eye level.

Elbows – over and under.

Arm circles – back and forward.

Waist – turning from side to side with head, torso and arms moving together.

Hip circling - feet shoulder-width and parallel.

Knee circling - knees together.

Sarpa - spinal movement.

Ankles

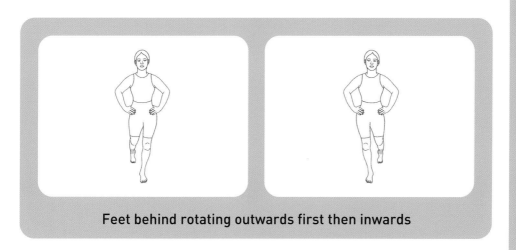

Feet behind rotating outwards first then inwards

Head and Neck

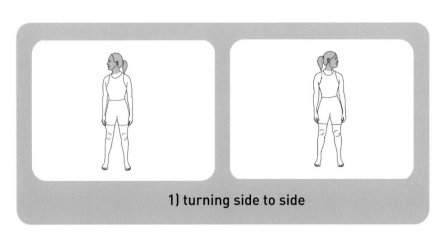

1) turning side to side

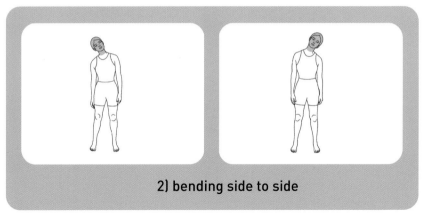

2) bending side to side

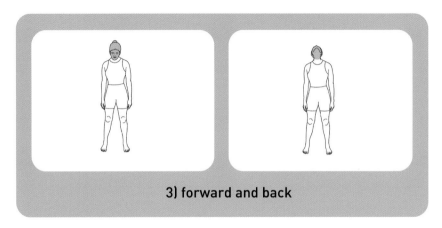

3) forward and back

Shoulders

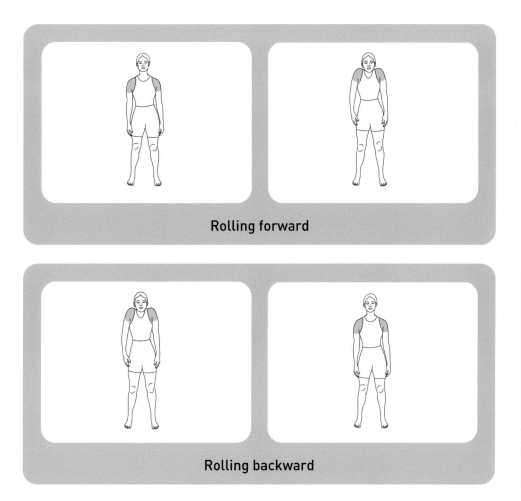

Rolling forward

Rolling backward

Wrist Circling

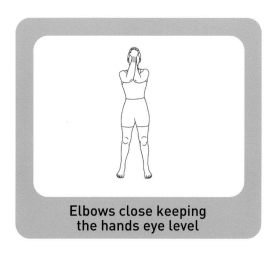

**Elbows close keeping
the hands eye level**

Elbows

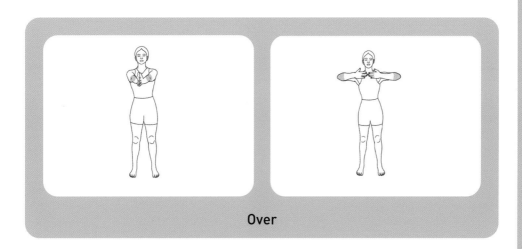

Over

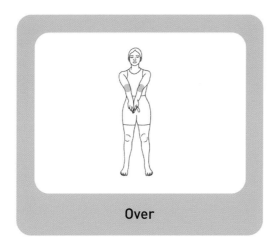

Over

Elbows

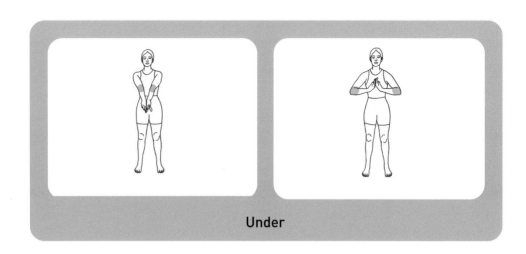

Under

Under

Arm Circles

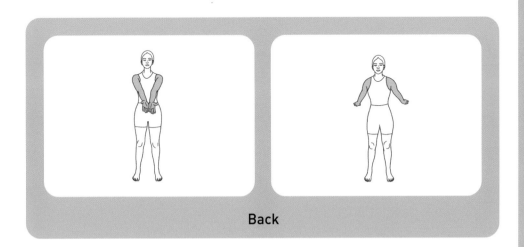

Back

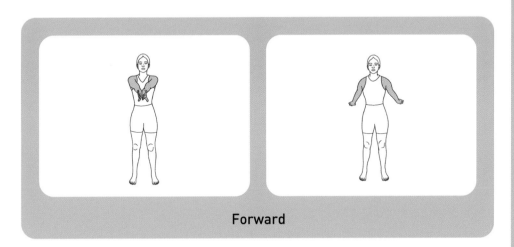

Forward

Waist

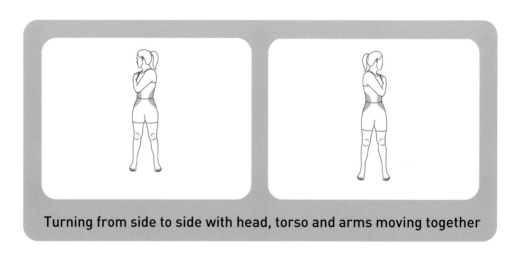

Turning from side to side with head, torso and arms moving together

Hip Circling

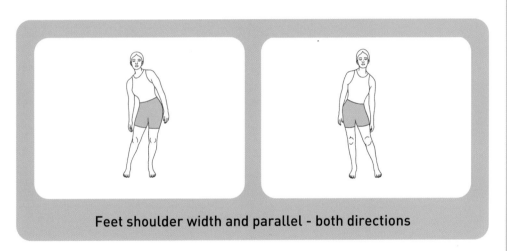

Feet shoulder width and parallel - both directions

Knee Circling

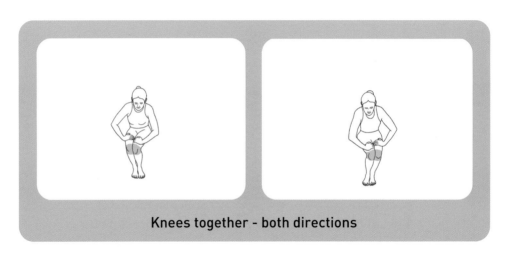

Knees together - both directions

Sarpa

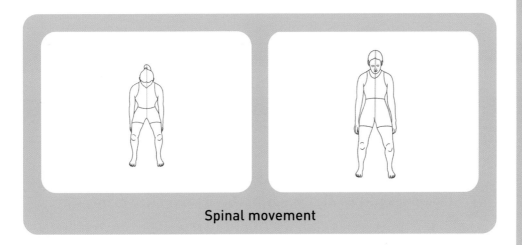

Spinal movement

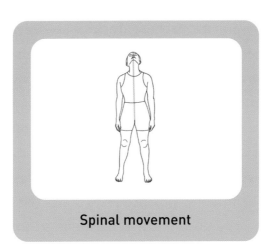

Spinal movement

The order of the movements is from the head to the feet after the initial rotation of the ankles which opens the hips and sets up a flow of energy to the feet.

Initially one can begin with 10 repetitions until a rhythm develops and one has memorised the sequence of movements. In the beginning, some of the movements are sometimes forgotten. It is better to continue, acknowledge the movement that was forgotten and then make a note to remember it next time. Returning to the movement that was forgotten will disturb the direction of the movements and the way the tension in the body is progressively released through this practice

Once the order of the *caraṇas* has been committed to memory, adding 5 movements each week until 50 repetitions are reached will take approximately 3 months. One exception to this is the head/neck movements. As there are three head/neck movements ie. side to side/forward & back etc, once 15-20 repetitions of the head/neck *caraṇas* are reached, this will be sufficient. For those suffering from low blood pressure 10 repetitions may be enough. Continuing this practice for a further three months will bring many improvements in joint mobility, circulation, digestion and breathing. It will also dramatically improve mental concentration and focus. The time for practice takes about the same number of minutes as the number of repetitions ie. 15 repetitions = 15 minutes.

Practice of these *caraṇas* develops awareness of the different parts of the body and will improve coordination. This coordination is focussed on the following joint pairs.

Hands and feet.

Wrists and ankles.

Elbows and knees.

Shoulders and hips.

These major joints belong to the outer structure of the physical body. They have corresponding parts that connect more internally. These are:

Palms of the hands and soles of the feet.

Inner wrists and inner ankles.

Inner crease of the elbows and backs of the knees.

Armpits and groin.

Through practice one learns not only the movements of the joints but how to connect more internally through these more delicate and sensitive areas. This is good for developing more refined coordination and deeper awareness in the practice.

Perhaps due to their apparent simplicity, the *caraṇas* are often overlooked in contemporary yoga yet they can yield profound benefits. As they are accessible to most people and are safe to practise they are excellent for getting into a routine of regular practice. Cultivating a regular practice, even with something as simple as the *caraṇas*, will yield many benefits. It will also make the practice of the stances and seats that follow much easier.

In performing the *caraṇas* there is no requirement to coordinate the breathing with the movements. One of the main functions of the *caraṇas* is to release the gross tensions in the body especially around the major joints so that when one does begin the coordination of breathing and movement it is much easier. This is introduced in the next stage with simple standing movements including squatting and lunging.

Tiptoe Balancing

Following the *caraṇas* one can raise and lower the heels with the feet together a number of times to prepare for balancing on the tiptoes. The tiptoe balance begins by lifting the heels and raising the arms out to the side and over the head while drawing the breath in. The heels are then lowered back to the floor and the arms and hands are brought down to the eyes and then down in front of the body with the exhalation. Balancing promotes focus and concentration. Keeping the feet and legs together requires an inward rotation of the legs which brings the focus to the centre. The tiptoe balance strengthens the lower back and improves overall posture by engaging the core muscles. For maximum benefit, the navel is kept slightly drawn back towards the spine and the shoulders are kept in line with the hips.

Coordination of the movements of the limbs with the breathing is introduced here. The arms are raised with the heels as the inhalation begins. The heels are lowered and the arms released down with the exhalation. However, there are two pauses in this sequence where there is no breathing and the breath is either held in or out for a brief period while the movement continues. As one begins to raise the arms from the side of the body the inhalation only begins at the point where one can feel the weight of the arms. This is usually at around a 45 degree angle from the body. It is at this point one begins the inhalation. So from the end of the exhalation until this point there is no breathing. Similarly at the end of the inhalation, when the arms are raised fully above the head and one is firmly balanced on the tiptoes, one first lowers the heels and begins to lower the arms while holding the breath in. The exhalation only begins once the arms/hands reach the level of the eyes and before the level of the chest. Thus one is introduced to the idea of there being 4 phases to the breathing: inhalation, pause, exhalation and pause. This is a natural breathing rhythm that should be established from the beginning. It has many applications at different stages of the yoga practice.

This focus on the breathing has proven to be incredibly beneficial for pregnant women. In over two decades of teaching pregnancy yoga I have been told countless times by women how much it supported them during labour, enabling them to remain relatively calm and focussed while giving birth. As a consequence, this has often led to a reduced level of intervention needed if difficulties arose during labour and the birth.

Additionally for pregnant women, this balancing movement on the tiptoes is excellent in supporting the lower back throughout the pregnancy. It can prevent and alleviate sciatica as well as stabilise the pubic symphysis later in the pregnancy.

Inhale and exhale and
hold the breath out.

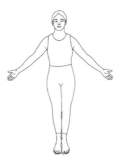

Raise the arms to the side to approx
45 degrees while holding the breath out.
Lift up on the heels at this point and
begin the inhalation.

Continue to raise the arms over the
head while inhaling, interlace the fingers
at the top and balance firmly on the toes.

While holding the breath in lower the
heels to the floor and then lower the
hands to eye level. Begin the exhale here.

Complete the exhale as you lower
the hands completely and repeat
from the beginning.

Squatting

Squatting is a natural movement yet many people have lost the ability to do so in modern times. There are a wide variety of squats and they can be dynamic or static. They can be practised at all levels from beginners to advanced. The three squats introduced here are tiptoe squats with the feet together, squats with the feet shoulder width apart, and with the feet one leg length apart. For the beginner, the progressive widening of the stances helps to memorise the order of movements. Squats promote flexibility in all of the joints of the lower limbs, the hips, knees and ankles. They tone all of the smaller muscles of the feet which support good posture, as well as the larger muscles of the legs and hips, including the calves, quadriceps, hamstrings, adductors and gluteal muscles.

Tiptoe Squats

Having strengthened the ankles and feet and developed focus and concentration through balancing on the toes, one is ready to learn the tiptoe squat.

It can be useful to use a wall for this balancing squat in the beginning. Start on the tiptoes with the hands held chest height with elbows straight or bent. Slowly bend the knees on the exhalation keeping the spine vertical and the heels raised. Maintain the connection with the navel towards the spine. Only go so far down that you maintain the resistance with the heels raised while the knees are bending. When it is no longer possible to maintain the lift of the heels when bending the knees it is at that point one should begin straightening the legs and come back up. Gradually one will be able to bend lower while maintaining the lift of the heels as well as maintaining the lift all the way on the way back up. As a general rule for squatting, exhalation is performed while bending and inhalation while straightening the legs.

This tiptoe squat builds strength in the legs and the core muscles of the body and gives mental focus. When performed correctly it is a very good movement for people who have suffered knee injuries and for those who have certain back conditions that require this kind of core strengthening.

Simple squat

The next movement is a simple squat with the feet shoulder-width apart. Squats are challenging for many people, especially for those who spend a lot of time sitting and working at a desk. However the benefits are many, especially in reducing tension around the hips and shoulders and in toning the muscles of legs. There are countless ways of doing these squats with different breathing rhythms and various combinations of static and dynamic arm movements.

In preparation for a squat, a one legged balance can be performed. While standing with the feet together lift the heel of the right foot off the floor while keeping the ball of the foot in contact with the floor. You will notice a shift in the weight towards the left foot. Maintaining the stability on the left foot, bend the right knee and lift the right leg up to the chest and hold the knee with the hands. Once the balance is steady you can slightly rotate the right hip inwards and bring the right foot towards the left hip while taking your right elbow around the knee to secure it. Hold the position for up to a minute and then repeat on the other side. This will stretch and release tension around the gluteal muscles as well as engage the adductors in preparation for the squats.

The squat is then performed with the feet shoulder-width apart and parallel. The feet should remain flat on the floor without the heels lifting. If needed, the feet can turn slightly outwards from parallel or be slightly wider than hip-width. On the inhalation, raise the arms out in front to chest level and focus the gaze of the eyes in between the hands, ie. roughly arm's-length. Have the wrists bent with the fingers pointing downwards. Holding the arms out in front helps with the balance during the squat. Once the arms are raised, start to bend the knees as you exhale, maintaining an upright spine as much as possible. Only go so far that you are able to keep your heels on the floor. In this way you will protect the knees. Keeping the arms extended out in front, come back up to standing, straightening the legs on the inhalation. Then relax the arms back down to the side on the exhalation. This is a simple version of the squat and gives a brief pause as the arms are lowered and raised in between each squat. To increase the intensity, maintain the raised arms throughout, without dropping them in between.

This squat promotes exhalation as the hips are lowered below the level of the knees and the breathing is forcefully expelled from the body. It releases tension from the hips and, as indicated earlier tones all the muscles of the legs. While it can be physically challenging to perform in the beginning, it will leave the practitioner mentally relaxed afterwards, as the emphasis on exhalation removes both physical and mental tension.

Squats promote elimination and they are a natural movement for defecation as well as for women during childbirth. However, due to our modern lifestyle, squats are difficult for most people and this contributes to many health problems including sluggish digestion, constipation and premenstrual tension. Most of these conditions are connected to a reduced function of elimination. Consequently unwanted material in the body not properly removed becomes a breeding ground for disease. This eliminating function is described in yogic terms as *apāna vāyu*, or the downward moving force in the body. Its main region in the body is in the lower abdominal region, including the large intestine, bladder and reproductive organs. It is also connected to the entire back region of the body, the base of the neck, coccyx and the heels.

As well as promoting elimination of waste from the body, *apāna vāyu* also removes negativity from the mind. This is easily observed after the practice of the squats, or other standing positions, when one feels mentally clearer and more relaxed. Over time, a daily yoga practice that includes squats and standing work can reduce tendencies towards depression and alleviate mood swings.

According to the ancient texts, many diseases arise due to weakened *apāna vāyu*. Conversely this also suggests that strengthening *apāna vāyu* can help improve many conditions.

Apāna vāyu is also considered to be an essential force in conception, carrying a child during pregnancy, as well as in the delivery of the child.

While squats are relatively simple movements, they can nevertheless have far reaching benefits for people in terms of physical health, mental well-being, and energetic balance. They provide much more than the largely inaccessible movements often used to promote yoga nowadays. Squats improve flexibility and cardiac fitness, digestion and elimination, breathing and

Standing with feet shoulder width
apart and parallel with arms
by the side. Exhale

Inhale. Raise the arms to chest level
with the wrists bent and fingers
pointing down.

Exhale and slowly bend the knees
keeping the feet flat and arms
extended in front.

Inhale. Come back up to standing.

Exhale. Release the arms back to the
side and repeat from the beginning.

mental equilibrium and particularly for women, menstrual and reproductive health.

Squats can also be done with simple arm movements to improve coordination and develop a dynamic rhythm between movement and breathing. Starting with the arms raised in front of the chest as mentioned earlier, a further variation is to then cross the arms over each other on an inhalation, squat down with the arms crossed over on the exhalation, come back up to standing on the inhalation and release the arms on the exhalation. This will deepen the benefits of the squats in releasing tension in the shoulders as well as the hips, and will engage the mind in a more complex rhythm of breathing and movement.

I recall once going to see an Ayurvedic doctor for the first time when I was living in Sydney, Australia. He did the normal Ayurvedic assessment of body type and constitution. He then proceeded to show me a simple squat which he performed with amazing grace and agility. I was quite taken aback and a little embarrassed as, although I had been practising yoga for more than five years, I was completely unable to squat. I had not encountered any of these simple kinds of squats in my yoga training. Not long after this, I began regularly practising this kind of simple squat. As I had encountered a few knee injuries and difficulties in the early stages of my yoga practice, I was very nervous about squatting. The instruction I followed was to perform 25 squats daily. I found after a few weeks the flexibility of my knees had improved considerably. The squatting hadn't added to my knee difficulties but had actually helped them!

A note of caution, however for those with more difficult knee injuries, the practice of these squats may require some adaptation with the help of a competent teacher.

Horse stance

This is a wider squat with the feet about one leg's-length apart and the feet turned to 45 degrees in which the hips only go down as low as the knees. This position can be physically demanding and builds strength.

Begin with the legs straight and the feet turned 45 degrees. Bring the attention to the four corners of the feet, namely the base of the big toes, little toes, inner and outer heels. Bend the knees from the space behind the knees so you feel the direction of movement from the hips towards the knees while keeping the weight even on the four corners of the feet. This is important as it is very common to simply drop into the hips and collapse the knees inwards. The spine should be kept as upright as possible.

The horse stance can be practised dynamically while holding the arms in a static position out in front, exhaling as you bend and inhaling as you straighten the legs and repeating this a number of times. It can also be practised coordinating the bending and straightening of the legs with different movements of the arms and the breathing. It can be held for periods of time to build strength. The horse stance is a basic position through which many of the warrior movements can be accessed as they are in the Shadow Yoga preludes.

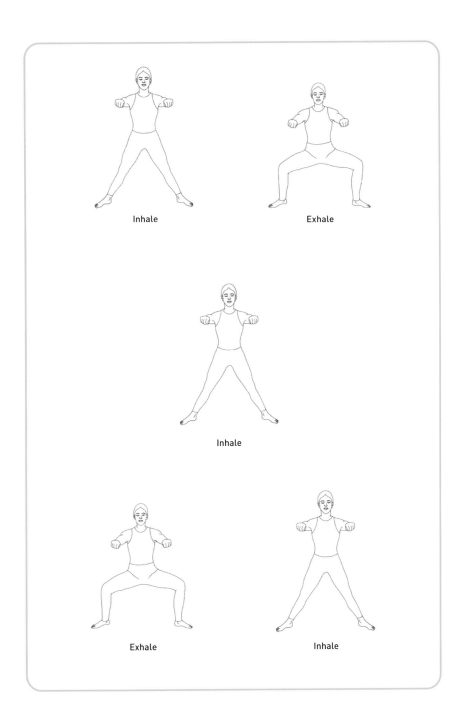

Inhale

Exhale

Inhale

Exhale

Inhale

Prasarita Padottanāsana

This position is a standing forward bend with straight legs one leg length apart and with the feet parallel. *Prasarita padottanāsana* literally translates as 'intense stretch with extended feet'. Initially most people do experience this forward bend as a strong stretch in the hamstrings. While keeping the outer edges of the feet parallel this position also promotes an inward rotation of the legs which tones the adductor muscles and releases tension in the gluteal muscles. This allows a deeper release and extension of the spine. It is generally practised as a static position and is often used to stabilise the focus and the breathing after more dynamic movements like the horse and warrior stances. There are a number of variations of this standing pose with different arm positions, twists and lateral movements of the torso. *Trikonāsana, parivṛtta trikonāsana* and *parsvottanāsana*, standing positions commonly found in yoga, are also incorporated into the standing sequences with *prasarita padottanāsana* in the third prelude of Shadow Yoga, *Kartikkeya Mandalam.*

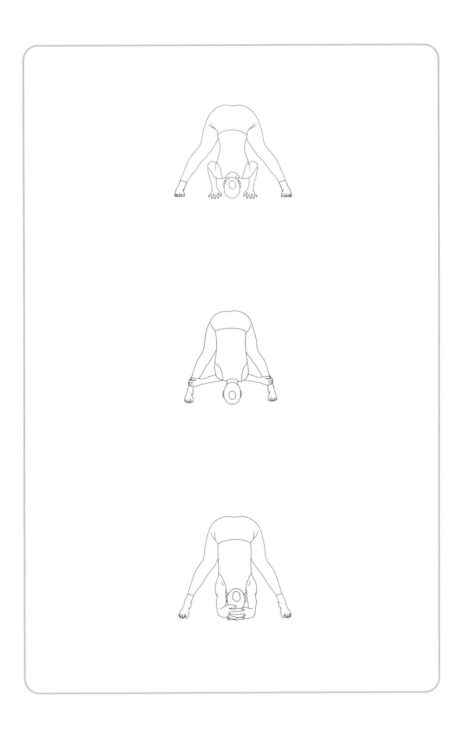

Skandasthana

Starting from *prasarita padottanāsana*, turn the feet to a 45 degree angle and hold the lower shins with the hands as close as possible to the ankles. Keep the elbow on the inner side of the knee, bend the leg and maintain the weight evenly on the four corners of the foot on the side you are bending towards. This can be achieved by bending from behind the knee as in the horse stance. Keep as much weight as possible on the straight leg foot on the floor. This prevents collapsing into the hip joint on the side you are bending to and keeps the movement central even though it is asymmetrical. This is the challenge of any asymmetrical position, how to keep the weight on the straight leg foot while bending the opposite leg. It is true of all the warrior movements of yoga where one leg is bent and the other leg is straight. Usually *skandasthana* is taught first bending down on one side with an exhalation and straightening the leg on the inhalation and then repeated on the other side. This sequence of dynamically alternating bending and straightening the legs with the breathing is repeated a number of times. A number of sets can be performed with *prasarita padottanāsana* in between to refocus the mind and stabilise the breathing. *Skandasthana* improves flexibility in the hips, knees and ankles and tones the hamstrings and adductors.

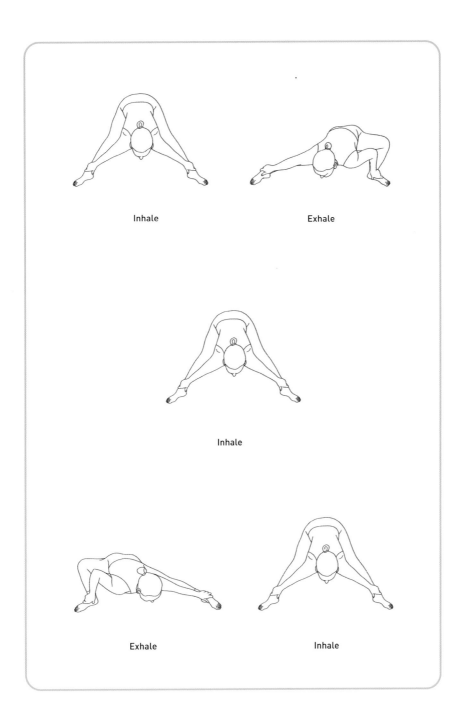

Inhale

Exhale

Inhale

Exhale

Inhale

This first stage of *skandasthana* is followed by progressively more challenging variations in the three preludes of Shadow Yoga and *Nrtta Sadhana.*

Summary

Together, these preliminary movements provide a first step in making a connection with the physical body, reducing stiffness and tension and in setting up a rhythm between movement and breath. For a complete beginner who has little or no experience of yoga this stage may take anywhere from 6 months to a year. They establish a sound foundation enabling one to proceed with confidence to the next stage of practice. Though the movements appear relatively simple, within them are hidden the keys that will unlock more complex activities. Even those who have prior experience of yoga will benefit.

Water

Seats

Circulation

Seats - *Āsana*

There are a number of different seated positions described in the yoga texts and many of these can be practiced from the beginning. Generally when both legs are bent in a seated posture these are referred to as seats. Having first performed the *caraṇas* and standing positions described in the previous chapter, the seats deepen the release of tension around the hips and shoulders as well improve the flexibility of the ankles and knees. They can be performed in an upright, forward and supine position. The upright positions lend themselves to breathing practices, with or without arm movements, as well as meditative activities. The forward bending variations focus the mind more internally, while the supine positions are more commonly used as restorative positions for deeper states of relaxation and to reduce tension in a more passive way. In terms of breathing, sitting upright has the effect of evening out the breathing so inhalation and exhalation are of the same duration. Bending forwards promotes exhalation and lying back promotes inhalation. Not only do these movements have different physical effects, they also influence the mental state. In yogic terminology these states are referred to as the *gunas* of *sattva*, *rajas* and *tamas* corresponding to clarity, excitability and inactivity respectively.

The seats can also be of the nature of inward rotation as in most kneeling positions, or outward rotation as in the lotus posture (*padmāsana*) or the cobbler's pose (*baddha konāsana*).

Mandukāsana - Frog Pose

This seat is the best for beginners to stabilise the breathing and circulation after the dynamic standing activity. It is also very good for runners and cyclists to release stiffness in the legs and hips. It is symmetrical and can be done forwards, upright and in a supine position with different arm and shoulder movements which can be both static and dynamic. There is also a mild twisting variation. *Mandukāsana* is relatively neutral in its rotation with the legs/knees at a 45 degree angle from the hips.

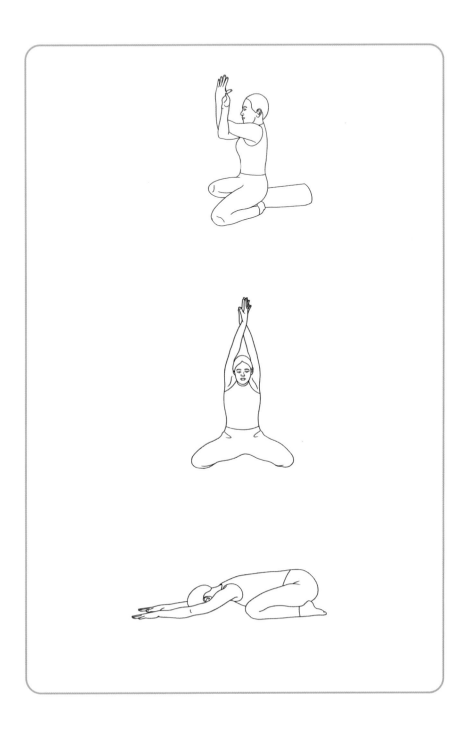

Sankatāsana - Dangerous Pose

Moving to a more inward rotation of the legs, *sankatāsana* is a more challenging seat for most people. It is asymmetrical with one leg placed under the other and it releases deeper layers of tension in the outer hips and gluteal muscles as well as in the groin. It can be performed with a variety of different arm movements also to release tension in the shoulders. There is also a twisting variation. Generally this position is performed in an upright position with some forward bending variations.

Vajrāsana - Thunderbolt Pose

A classic kneeling position with both knees together and with the hips between the heels, this seat is symmetrical and inward rotating. It has a deep effect on the groin area as well as improving circulation in the legs and is particularly good for pregnant women to help in the prevention of varicose veins. This seat can be performed with a variety of static arm movements to release tension in the shoulders as well as dynamic arm movements to improve the breathing. It can also be performed sitting upright, bending forwards and lying backwards. For some people, it may be necessary to use a support in the seated or supine variations. It is also a seat that can be used for the cultivation of *uḍḍiyāna bandha* (see Chapter 4) due to the natural grip it invokes in the lower abdominal region.

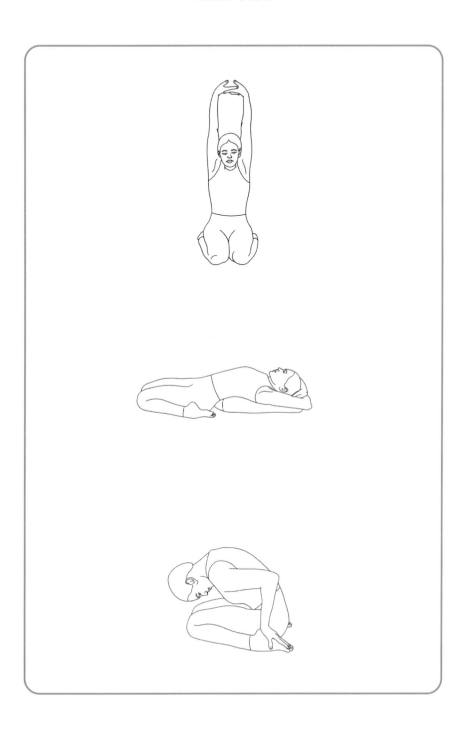

Sukhāsana - Comfortable/Easy Pose

Commonly referred to as crossed legs, this asymmetrical seat is generally the easiest of the outward rotating positions and the position most people adopt when sitting on the ground. In the early stages, some people may need to use a support under their hips in this position until some of the tension in the hips begins to release. This is a seat which can be done sitting upright combined with different arm and shoulder movements to release tension in the shoulders and in the joints of the arms and hands. It can be practiced bending forwards to deepen the release of tension and in a supine position as a restorative practice and a more passive release of tension. In the upright position, it also has a number of twisting variations. *Sukhāsana* is a seat which can also be used for breathing practices, cultivation of the *bandhas*, and meditative activities in cases where *padmāsana* is not possible.

Baddha Konāsana - Cobbler's Pose or Bound Angle Pose

An outwardly rotating symmetrical seat that releases tension in the hips and groin region. This seat is particularly good for women especially during the menstrual cycle and pregnancy. It has its upright, forward bending and supine variations. It is a particularly good seat for practising pelvic floor exercises. It is not usually used for meditative activities.

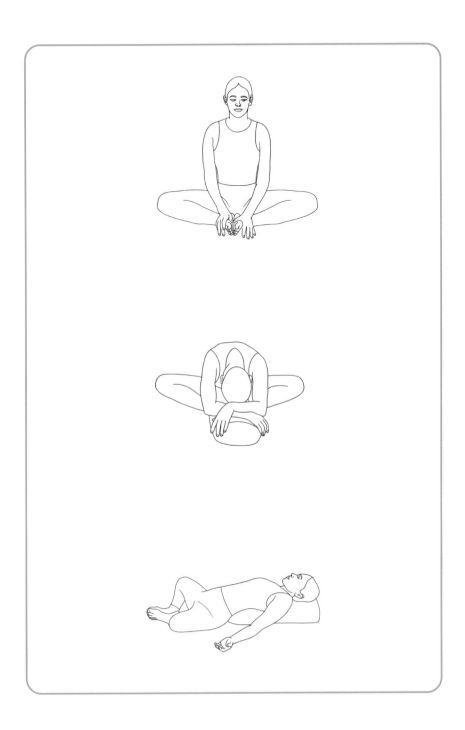

Padmāsana - Lotus Posture

This is an outward rotating asymmetrical *āsana* where one leg is placed over the other with the feet placed on the thighs near the groin. The groin and sinus regions are very closely connected and placement of the first foot on the groin will block the sinus on that side causing the opposite nostril to open. For this reason, during the practice of *prānāyāma*, the right leg is usually placed in first to block the left groin/sinus and open the right nostril. The hatha yoga texts describe three main channels or *nādis*, *idā* on the left side, *pingala* on the right side and *susumnā* in the centre. Ida *nādi* is said to correspond to the moon and is cooling, *pingala* to the sun and therefore heating, and *susumnā* to fire. By blocking the left nostril and opening the right this increases the heat in the body and purifies the *nādis* (energetic channels). It is mentioned in the yoga texts that the purification of the *nādis* is essential for the energy to flow more freely in the body. This purification of the *nādis*, known as *nādi śuddhi*, is usually the first stage in the preparatory practices towards *prānāyāma*.

Padmāsana is one of two seats recommended in the yoga texts for the deeper meditative activities due to its effect of maintaining the uprightness of the spine. It too can be performed upright, bending forwards and in a supine variation. In later stages it has a wide number of variations.

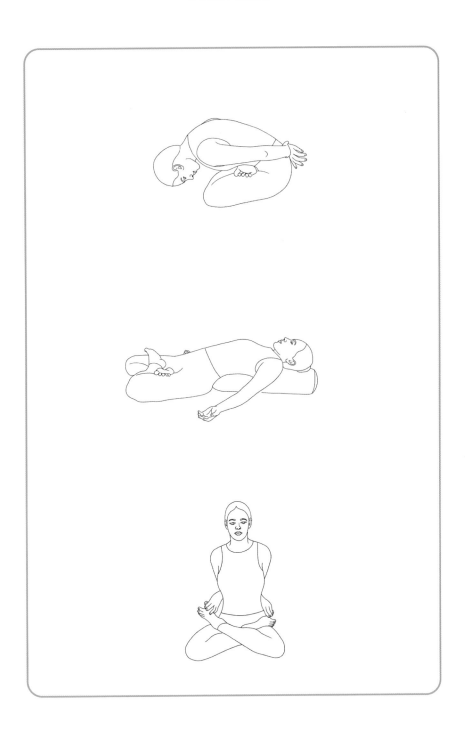

Practising *āsana*

These basic seats have varying functions and can be practised in a number of different sequences and arrangements with forward, upright and supine positions within a single practice session. In the beginning stages, the seats provide balance and a period of recovery after the dynamic standing activity. As mentioned earlier, the frog pose (*mandukāsana*) and its variations are excellent positions for this, stabilising the breathing and circulation. With experience one becomes aware of how to use different seated variations for overcoming different physical and mental tensions. In the later stages, the seated positions become a key part of the breathing and meditative practices. In the standing activity, rhythm is established through larger, more dynamic movements; in the seated work, however, coordination with the breath is achieved through smaller movements, thus refining the concentration and awareness. Different arrangements of seats within a practice are called *āsana-aṅgahāra*.

Fire

Uḍḍiyāna
Bandha

Digestion

Fire: *Uḍḍiyāna Bandha*

Bandhas

Bandhas are deep and internal practices frequently mentioned in the hatha yoga texts. Three *bandhas* are commonly described: *jālandhāra bandha, uḍḍiyāna bandha* and *mūla bandha*, corresponding to the throat, navel and perineal floor respectively. Knowledge of these *bandhas* is considered essential if the deeper practices of yoga are to yield their benefits. They require skill and attentiveness and it is recommended that they are learnt under guidance from someone who has a good understanding of them. The teacher must observe the student carefully to avoid any negative side effects. For a beginner, learning the *bandhas* will bring many benefits including improved mental focus, digestion and elimination as well as establish a good breathing rhythm. They can also contribute to improved posture. *Uḍḍiyāna bandha* is the most accessible in the beginning and for this reason it is the one that will be discussed here.

Uḍḍiyāna Bandha

The literal meaning of *uḍḍiyāna* is to fly upwards and *bandha* is derived from the Sanskrit verb *bandh* which means to bind, tie, fix or fasten. Thus *uḍḍiyāna bandha* literally means the 'upward flying bind', however, in practice, this literal translation leads easily to misinterpretation as we will soon discuss.

Uḍḍiyāna bandha is performed at the end of the exhalation and while holding the breath out. The abdomen is then drawn back completely towards the spine. Most descriptions state that the abdomen should be drawn equally back above and below the navel. Apart from this there is little practical information available to a beginner. *Nathamuni's Yoga Rahasya*, a twentieth century text by T. Krishnamacarya, gives a good outline of the process required as well as a description of its benefits. In learning *uḍḍiyāna bandha* it is stated that before practising any kind of breath retention one must first learn to inhale and exhale evenly. Only then will one be able to retain the breath without undue imposition and stress. In the case of *uḍḍiyāna bandha,* a stress-free exhalation retention is required together with an ability to inhale smoothly after its release. This is a skill that takes time and which can be developed by the practices that promote the coordination of the body movements and the breath outlined in this book. It is progressively developed in the Shadow Yoga preludes.

Incorrect practice of *uḍḍiyāna bandha* can lead to negative side effects including headaches, pressure in the heart and lungs and problems with the eyes and ears. These side effects are often caused by excessive lifting of the diaphragm due to the misunderstanding of the term 'flying upwards'. Even when the instruction 'equally draw back above and below the navel' is acknowledged, applying it in practice can be difficult. It is generally easier to draw the upper abdomen back (above the navel) than it is to draw the lower abdomen back (below the navel). Inevitably this will lead to the upper abdomen being drawn back more in the early stages of practice, due to inexperience and unfamiliarity with the movement. This will not create problems if it is corrected but if *uḍḍiyāna bandha* is habitually practiced this way problems can develop. On this note, people who suffer from high or low blood pressure are advised against practising *uḍḍiyāna bandha* as it can exacerbate either condition.

The term 'flying upwards' does not refer to the gross physical movement of lifting the abdominal organs upwards. It refers instead to the subtle internal movement of the *prāna* (or life force) upwards through the *suṣumnā nāḍi* - the central channel within the spine. This is a deep internal movement and is the outcome of many years of refinement in the yoga practice. It is a process that cannot be forced but is arrived at. In many texts it is made clear that before the *prāna* moves upwards it must first be concentrated at the base of the spine. Hence the requirement to equally draw back above and below the navel. Practised in this manner, unwanted side effects are avoided and *uḍḍiyāna bandha* will also strengthen *apāna vāyu*, the downward or eliminating force in the body.

A number of less well known benefits of *uḍḍiyāna bandha* are described in the *Yoga Rahasya*. These include improved menstruation and female reproductive health. This is primarily due to the strengthening of *apāna vāyu* and improved circulation in the lower abdominal region. I have often observed such benefits in women after teaching them *uḍḍiyāna bandha*. Here it should be noted that while *uḍḍiyāna bandha* is particularly beneficial for women it should not be practiced during menstruation, pregnancy, nor while breastfeeding. In recent years, the subject of women's health has gained more attention but many negative stereotypes and attitudes persist. Acknowledging and respecting the menstrual cycle and natural rhythms of the body is an integral part of the yoga practice. Yoga practice needs to be adapted during menstruation, pregnancy and menopause. There are general guidelines to be followed in each of these cases but these may need to be modified according to the individual and their circumstances.

Correct practice of *uḍḍiyāna bandha* also strengthens the digestive power known in yoga as *agni*. *Agni* works on many layers beginning with the primary power of digestion in the small intestine called *jaṭhara-agni*. Digestion occurs throughout all the layers of tissues in the body which are termed *dhātus*. There are seven *dhātus* starting from the most gross layer, that of the digestion of food *rasa*, to the most refined layer, the reproductive tissue, *śukra*. There is also a process of digestion for each of the five elements, or the *bhūta-agni*, corresponding to earth (*pṛthvī*), water (*ap*), fire (*tejas*), air (*vāyu*) and space (*ākāśa*). In total, 13 types of *agni* are described, all dependent on *jaṭhara-agni*. If this basic power of digestion is weak it will lead to imbalances in digestion and absorption of nutrients throughout all the tissues of the body, creating the conditions for disease.

The practice of *uḍḍiyāna bandha* strengthens the digestion firstly by the direct physical massage of the digestive organs and second by improving the circulation to them thus removing sluggishness and stagnation. Together with appropriate diet, this contributes to maintaining the health of the whole body. *Mitāhāra* is the term used in yoga to describe appropriate diet and it refers to things such as eating in rhythm with the seasons, according to one's constitution and to the requirements of the body. Recent scientific studies have shown how much the gut and digestive health affects the mind and mental states. Thus, improving digestive power through *uḍḍiyāna bandha* will also benefit mental health. On another level, all experiences in life need to be digested and assimilated. *Agni* and *mitāhāra* also relate to the digestion of these experiences. It is common to have 'undigested' experiences in the mind which can lead to unconscious behaviour or chronic conditions. Learning to breathe evenly while paying attention to the pauses between each breath slows down the mind and allows these unconscious 'undigested' or unassimilated experiences to then come to the surface. They can then be resolved or integrated accordingly.

So as not to disturb the digestion it is always recommended that *uḍḍiyāna bandha* is practised on an empty stomach. After completing an exhalation, one should hold the breath out and equally draw the abdomen back above and below the navel. After releasing the abdomen, one should inhale smoothly without jerkiness or gasping. It takes time to achieve this. It is necessary to be patient and not force the breathing or hold the breath out longer than one is comfortably able. One will quickly learn to recognise one's limits in this regard. It is common in the early stages to experience some gasping with the inhalation after releasing the *uḍḍiyāna bandha* but this will ease with practice. The inhalation becomes increasingly smooth as one learns to maintain a slight contraction of the navel as one releases the *bandha*. This contraction of the navel is an inherent and natural part of breathing that most people lose after early childhood due to accumulated tensions and conditioning.

Drawing the navel back

Described below is a simple practice to restore the natural power hidden within the breathing process

1. Lie on the back with both knees bent and the feet placed on the floor shoulder-width apart. With the hands resting on the lower belly, feel the rise and fall of each breath during inhalation and exhalation respectively.

2. After a while the breathing will slow down and one will become aware of the pauses occurring between each breath. At the end of the exhalation, the abdomen will be relaxed.

3. At this point, at the end of the exhalation, continue to relax further into the lower abdomen. Repeat this for a number of breaths. A natural contraction of the navel towards the spine will be felt.

4. Maintain this contraction of the navel during the inhalation while remaining relaxed. Gradually the pressure from the inhalation will be felt more in the back and sides of the body, particularly in the lower back and the back of the ribs, and not just in the front of the abdomen and chest.

5. The key here is to remain relaxed while maintaining the natural contraction of the navel towards the spine and not to grip the navel or hold it back by force.

6. It will be clear if there is imposition from the mind. The breathing will become more shallow, there will be less pressure felt in the back and sides and more pressure in the front of the body.

7. An understanding of this connection between the inhalation and the navel being drawn back is required in order to inhale correctly after the release of *uḍḍiyāna bandha*.

With this lying down practice, it is also easy to observe the effect of the position of the neck and the throat on the movement of breath in the body. If the neck is contracted with the chin pulled up it will be difficult to maintain the evenness of the breath in the back and the sides of the body. The pressure from the breathing will be experienced more in the front of the body. This can be due either to restrictions in the physical posture, particularly in the neck and shoulders, or from tension held in the space of the throat, or both. By becoming aware of this and making adjustments, one gradually learns about the practice of *jālandhāra bandha*. Similarly, while maintaining the natural contraction of the navel towards the spine at the end of the exhalation, one will notice a spontaneous lifting of the pelvic floor during the inhalation. This is the beginning of the cultivation of the *bandha* at the perineum, *mūla bandha*. Many yoga texts state that the correct practice of *uḍḍiyāna bandha* helps in cultivating these other two *bandhas*. The cultivation of the three *bandhas* is essential for *prāṇāyāma* (often translated as breath control) and the deeper practices described in the hatha yoga texts. Without them those practices will yield few if any benefits.

Practising Uḍḍiyāna Bandha

In the beginning stages, it is good to learn *uḍḍiyāna bandha* towards the end of the practice when a good breathing rhythm has been established. It can be practised lying down so that it is easier to relax and allow the breathing to slow down. This also encourages the abdomen to relax towards the spine as well as making it easier to feel when the breathing moves into the back of the body with the inhalation, as the back is in contact with the ground. Once familiar with the complete process of exhalation, *uḍḍiyāna bandh*a, release of the *uḍḍiyāna*, and then inhalation, *uḍḍiyāna bandha* can be performed at the beginning of the practice to set up a good breathing rhythm. It can then be incorporated into the stance work and the seated activity. This will develop good focus and concentration in the yoga practice. There are some positions that lend themselves to the practice of *uḍḍiyāna bandha* and others where it is more difficult. Illustrated here is a standing sequence for practising *uḍḍiyāna bandha* at the beginning of the practice showing the appropriate coordination between breathing and movement.

1. Standing with feet shoulder width apart. Relax with the arms by the side. Exhale.

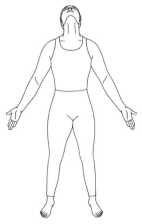

2. Holding the breath out, take the head back and raise the arms about 45 degrees. At that point begin to inhale.

3. While inhaling raise the arms completely above the head.

4. Hold the breath in and lower the hands level with the eyes.

5. Continue to hold the breath in and bring the hands to the top of the thighs.

6. Begin to exhale while bending the knees and slide the hands down to just above the knees. Keep the spine straight.

7. While holding the breath out draw the abdomen back equally above and below the navel. *Uḍḍiyāna bandha.*

8. While holding the *uḍḍiyāna bandha* come back to standing. Relax the *uḍḍiyāna bandha* and breathe in or repeat from step 1.

Air

Prāna Mudrā

Breathing

Air: Breathing

Breathing

Without food the human body can survive for weeks and even months, without water a few days, but without air we can only survive a few minutes. It is clear breathing is essential for life. We have evolved to breathe without having to think about it, whether we are awake or asleep as breathing is regulated by the autonomic nervous system. The mechanical process of breathing is relatively straightforward. The diaphragm is a muscular and fibrous dome shaped structure that separates the thoracic cavity or chest from the abdominal cavity. During inhalation it contracts and flattens, increasing the volume in the thoracic cavity, reducing the pressure and thus creating a vacuum in the lungs. This leads to the outside air being drawn in in order to equalise the pressure. During exhalation the diaphragm relaxes back into the thoracic cavity and due to the resulting increase in pressure, air is then pushed out of the lungs.

Physiologically our breathing can be influenced by a number of factors, many of which allow us to respond quickly to our environment. When oxygen is needed for muscular activity the heart rate increases to pump more blood and oxygen to the tissues and to remove carbon dioxide and breathing becomes faster. Concentration often leads to people unconsciously holding their breath as they focus their mental energy. Fear can set off a cascade of hormonal reactions which can trigger panic attacks and short shallow breathing. Stress can also lead to disturbances in the natural process of breathing. Different emotional states, both acute and chronic, can affect breathing patterns. Tension in the body from poor posture restricts breathing in many people. Lack of movement and exercise also reduces lung capacity. Thus, while breathing is an essential part of life, physically relatively simple in its action, a range of physiological and psychological factors can influence the depth and quality of breathing.

Thus two things that are most relevant in the yoga practice when considering the breathing are bodily structure, including posture and physical tension, and mental outlook or attitude. As well as physical tension, chronic tension from suppressed emotions such as fear, anxiety and anger can also impact the ability to breathe fully. Part of the process of developing a yoga practice involves becoming aware of such tensions and reducing them. We can gradually disentangle the breath from these restrictions and develop a deeper, more conscious connection between the body, mind and breath. This takes time and patience and can be immensely challenging and rewarding in equal measure.

To begin with, the *caraṇas* provide many benefits by reducing physical restrictions in the body which impede breathing. These are followed by the preparatory squats, lunges and forward bending movements that are coordinated with the breathing to further release tension especially around the shoulders and hips. With correct positioning and alignment these movements develop a posture that supports good breathing by integrating the upper and lower body through the centre. Because the standing and leg work is physically dynamic it is easy to bring the focus to the breathing. Having made a connection to the breathing rhythm, the next step is to refine the awareness and focus on the breath. This is achieved through learning to coordinate arm movements and breathing.

Prāna Mudrā

Yoga practices that coordinate movements of the arms with breathing are referred to as *prāna mudrā*. *Prāna* refers to the energy, or *vāyu*, corresponding to the upper region of the torso, above the diaphragm that includes the heart and the lungs and *mudrā*, in this instance, refers to gestures made with the hands. I have found it to be one of the most simple and at the same time most challenging practices for many people. It introduces an important element in the yoga practice for beginners as well as cultivating a deeper and more intuitive awareness that is necessary for the more internal practices of *prāṇāyāma* and meditation that come later. There are many variations of *prāṇa mudrā* involving different arm movements and patterns of breathing. A simple sequence of arm movements is presented here as a first step.

Two features of this sequence are key to their efficacy. First the arms are kept below the level of the shoulders and second, the movements are circular. Many people carry tension in the shoulders and neck due to mental stress or from working for long periods of time at a desk or on computers. In common yoga practices like the sun salutations or in the dog pose where the arms are raised or held above the head, such tension in the shoulders commonly manifests as difficulty in straightening the arms. In the beginning it is extremely difficult to release this kind of tension in these positions.

Keeping the arm movements below the level of the shoulders means those muscles that are holding the tension are not being lifted up further. The circular nature of the arm movements tones all the muscles around the neck and shoulders and thus removes tension that is held there. Furthermore keeping the wrists bent and extending from the elbows to the wrists during the movements will draw tension out of the shoulders. All the joints in the arm then work together to perform the movement, reducing the stress on any one part of the arm or shoulder.

This connection between the wrists and the elbows can be used in many other movements to reduce tension and over-reliance on the shoulders. This strengthens all the joints in the arms, improves the function of the heart and lungs, and deepens the breathing. It also brings more sensitivity to the hands and fingers. In yoga the hands are considered as belonging to the air element and to the sense of touch and feeling.

In the beginning it is easier to practise *prāna mudrā* with simple inhalation and exhalation. Extra breaths may be required until one has grasped the feeling and shapes of the movements. A common difficulty encountered initially is that while concentrating on learning the movements, people hold their breath and forget when to breathe in and out. Alternatively when they do remember to breathe they forget the sequence of the movements. This can be frustrating but is quite normal in the beginning and can be challenging even for those with experience of yoga.

Once the coordination of movement and breathing is grasped, the number of movements performed on each breath can be increased. The breathing will become slower and the pauses between each breath will naturally lengthen. Movements can also be performed in these pauses. Being able to coordinate the movements of the arms with the breathing prepares one for learning the more complex coordination between the movements of the arms and the legs with the breathing. Together with correct positioning, this integrates the upper and lower body and it is this integration that is progressively developed through the preludes of Shadow Yoga.

Though these movements are relatively simple, they can have

deep and profound effects. It is mentioned in some texts that *prāna vāyu*, the energy corresponding to the upper region of the torso, also governs memory. When I began my yoga teaching apprenticeship I had little training in physical movement. My main exercise activities were cycling, swimming and working out at the gym. I was completely unable to remember arrangements of movements and the connections between different shapes. Two women who were training with me at the same time had been professional dancers and I was in awe of their ability to remember sequences of movement. The first years of my yoga training did not include any breathing practices or any coordination of arm movements and breathing. It was focused primarily on correct positioning and alignment of the body and holding poses for long periods of time. Though I improved physically in terms of flexibility and my ability to perform various kinds of postures, my ability to remember sequences of movements hardly changed. When I was introduced to Shadow Yoga, a striking difference was the use of the arms in the flow and rhythm of the movements. I began practising some simple arm movements with the breathing and started coordinating them with the movements of my legs. After about a year, I noticed that while observing a sequence of movements one day I could spontaneously remember the order of those movements. It was quite an Aha! moment. I was intrigued. Quite independently, my teacher Sundernath observed a similar phenomenon. He had conducted a two year teacher training course and had introduced this type of coordination in the first year. He observed that the people who had practised what he had taught over the first year had improved their capacity for this type of memory and learning. These observations marked a turning point in my appreciation of the potential of yoga to transform the mind. The power of simple movements to elicit such a deep and tangible change in the mind was completely unexpected. There seemed to be no logical connection between the two things.

Prāna mudrā has also been found to be very beneficial for asthmatics. The arm movements strengthen the heart and lungs without the person needing to focus directly on the breathing. By paying attention to the movements of the hands and arms instead, this bypasses the fear which can often arise for people with asthma when performing breathing exercises.

For the majority of people looking for a way to mentally relax, or for those wishing to engage in deeper meditative activities, it is very difficult, if not impossible to focus solely on the breathing in the beginning. The beauty of these movements is that they give the mind a very tangible object to focus on, ie. the movement of the arms. Once the mind is engaged in this way, the attention can then be directed towards the breath without the support of the arms. The movements redirect the mind's attention away from thinking to the sense of touch and feeling and subsequently change the rhythm within the mind. While teaching the arm movements, I have observed that when students are asked to perform them by themselves and make mistakes they know because they recognize the feeling is different. In the beginning people often try to think about what to do but that is quickly superseded by feeling what to do. The unique benefit of *prāna mudrā* lies in promoting this intuitive awareness.

This intuitive faculty is particularly pronounced in women during pregnancy and the *prāna mudrā* is a great boon for women at this time. As the baby grows and the breasts become heavier, tension accumulates around the shoulders and neck and these movements specifically target this kind of tension and can reduce the incidence of carpal tunnel syndrome, a common condition in pregnant women. In the same way this sequence is very beneficial for nursing mothers in reducing the similar neck and shoulder issues that arise from breastfeeding. The mental space that is created in the movements through the breathing also gives breastfeeding mothers a valuable tool in combating post-natal depression and the fatigue that can come from the demands of a newborn child and the adjustments to motherhood. On a final note, when practised during pregnancy *prāna mudrā* develops strength in the arms that will prove invaluable while carrying and nursing the child. This is a very specific strength imparted by the coordination of all the joints in the arms that no other movement gives. I recall a student once who was very keen on practising the *prāna mudrā* throughout her pregnancy. After her child was born she returned to class and told me her husband could not carry the child for more than a few minutes at a time. She was surprised as she had no such difficulty. When I mentioned that

Begin with arms extended out
in front with palms up. Inhale.

Bend wrists up and
draw hands to hips. Exhale.

Turn hands back and extend backwards
(wrists still flexed). Inhale, bringing hands
round to the side peripheral vision and hold.
Exhale.

Bring hands back behind body with arms
extended and then bending the elbows bring
the hands to hips. Inhale.

Turn hands up and push hands
forward. Exhale.

Repeat from beginning 3-5 rounds.

Continue from end of first movement
with arms/hands forward. Pick up hands
with wrists bent, fingers pointing down.
Inhale.

Take arms out to the side straight and
level with shoulders. Inhale.

Turn hands. Exhale.

Extend arms behind the back
and then bending the elbows bring
the hands to hips. Inhale.

Turn hands and push hands forward.
Exhale.

Repeat from beginning 3-5 rounds.

this was one of the benefits of *prāna mudrā* described in the yoga texts it made complete sense.

Further practice

Once one has established a good rhythm with the *prāna mudrā* it is possible to insert the static arm positions of *Vahni* and *Gomukhāsana* in between cycles of the *prāna mudrā*. This will make these positions more accessible and will allow a deeper release to take place while holding them as the breathing will flow more freely. As tensions release, one starts to notice a different level of coordination within the static positions where smaller, more refined movements can be coordinated with the breathing.

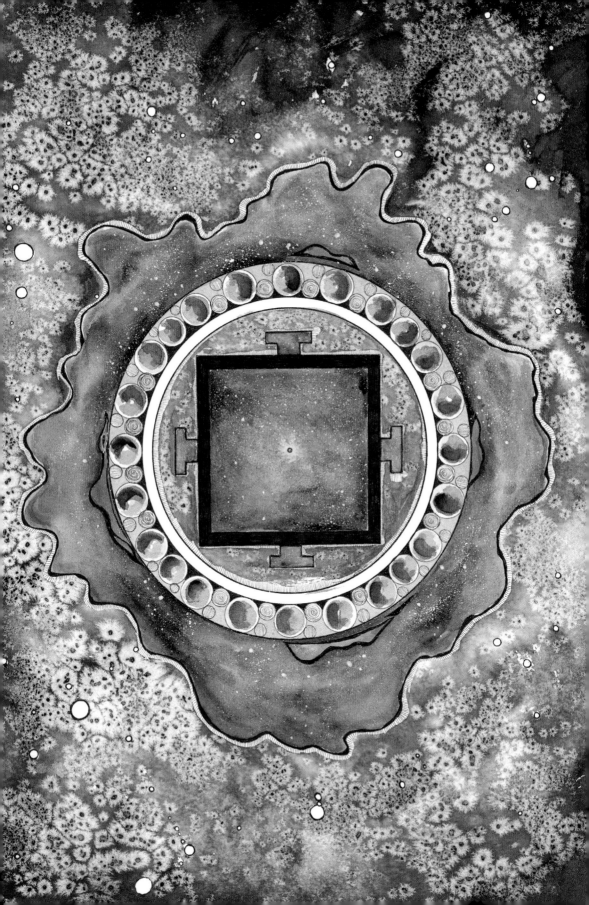

Space

Ādhāras

Concentration

Space: Concentration

Dṛṣṭi - Focus

A steady focus or gaze is a prerequisite for a steady mind. In yoga, the point of focus used to achieve this is called *dṛṣṭi*. For a beginner the best point to focus on is along the side of the nose, towards the tip, and approximately one arm's length away. To bring the focus to this point it is helpful to place the tip of the tongue to the point behind the two front teeth. Here there is a small protrusion of the gums where the tongue can be held. When the tongue is held here and the eyes rest along the side of the nose, the focus of the mind is maintained throughout the yoga practice. While it may be necessary to keep bringing the focus back to this point when the mind becomes distracted, it is important that the focus is relaxed and not forced.

Pratyāhāra - Sense withdrawal

In the descriptions of the stages of yoga there is a clear differentiation between practices that are more external, such as bodily activity or *āsana*, and those that are more internal such as concentration (*dhārana*) and meditation (*samādhi*). The bridge between these is called *pratyāhāra* which is often translated as the withdrawal of the senses. Once a rhythm has been established with the breath and the movement, this rhythm can be turned inwards to begin this process. This is achieved by focussing on a series of points in the body. These are sixteen points that run along the midline of the body from the tips of the big toes to the top of the head. They correspond to vital organs like the heart and bladder and other important areas including the navel and perineum. These points are called *ādhāras* (supporting junctions) as they are the locations of organs or structures that support the life of the body, either on a gross physical level or an internal energetic level, or both.

The 16 *Ādhāras*

1. Big toes	*Padaṅguṣṭhādhāra*
2. Perineum	*Mulādhāra*
3. Anus	*Gudādhāra*
4. Root of genitals	*Meḍhrādhāra*
5. Bladder	*Oḍḍīyānādhāra*
6. Navel	*Nabhyādhāra*
7. Heart	*Hṛdayādhāra*
8. Root of the throat	*Kaṇṭhādhāra*
9. Uvula	*Ghaṇṭikādhāra*
10. Hard palate	*Talvādhāra*
11. Tip of tongue	*Jihvādhāra*
12. Between the eyebrows	*Bhrūmadhyādhāra*
13. Tip of the nose	*Nasādhāra*
14. Root of the nose	*Nasāmūlakaptādhāra*
15. Middle of the forehead	*Lalatādhāra*
16. Crown of the head	*Brahmarandhrādhāra*

Five Elements of Hatha Yoga

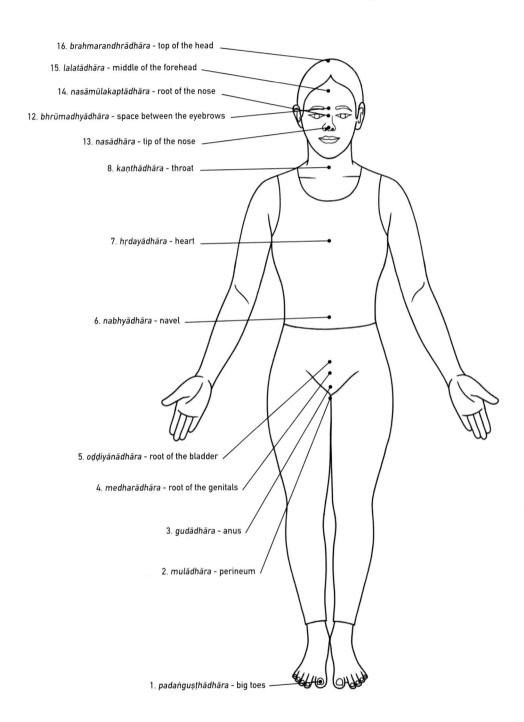

16. *brahmarandhrādhāra* - top of the head

15. *lalatādhāra* - middle of the forehead

14. *nasāmūlakaptādhāra* - root of the nose

12. *bhrūmadhyādhāra* - space between the eyebrows

13. *nasādhāra* - tip of the nose

8. *kaṇṭhādhāra* - throat

7. *hṛdayādhāra* - heart

6. *nabhyādhāra* - navel

5. *oḍḍiyānādhāra* - root of the bladder

4. *medharādhāra* - root of the genitals

3. *gudādhāra* - anus

2. *mulādhāra* - perineum

1. *padaṅguṣṭhādhāra* - big toes

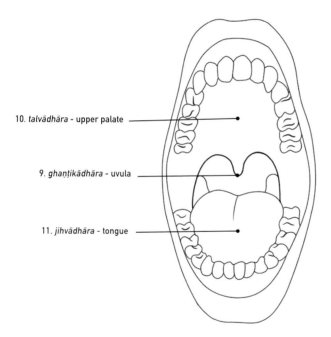

10. *talvādhāra* – upper palate

9. *ghaṇṭikādhāra* – uvula

11. *jihvādhāra* – tongue

To begin, first one needs to stabilise the breathing. Then on the exhalation take the attention of the mind to the first *ādhāra*, the big toes and then hold the attention on that area while breathing in. After the inhalation the attention is taken to the next *ādhāra* on the exhalation and so on until the point at the top of the head is reached.

Pratyāhāra can be done in a number of different positions. The simplest is with both feet together on the ground, holding the arms in front of the chest as if holding a big beach ball. This is called *stambha* or 'immovable pillar' which suggests the inner firmness or steadiness of mind that should be cultivated. A more challenging variation can be done standing on one leg in the tree pose (*vṛkṣāsana*) with the hands placed on the chest or on the top of the head in different hand positions.

These variations can be done after some preliminary movements where the breathing rhythm is established to internalise the focus on the rhythm, or when one is more familiar with focussing on the breath, they can be done at the start of the yoga practice to create a more internal focus from the beginning.

Pratyāhāra can also be done at the very end of the practice during relaxation in the corpse pose (*śavāsana*). While lying down in itself is seen by most people to be the most relaxing part of the yoga practice, in the yoga texts *śavāsana* is considered to be an extremely difficult pose to master. This is because it is very difficult to maintain mental alertness while completely relaxing the body. *Pratyāhāra* practiced here helps to develop this concentration.

Later on, *pratyāhāra* in *śavāsana* is used as a preliminary before *prāṇāyāma* or other internal yoga practices. As is often the case, practices that are used at the end of one stage, extracting the essence from what has gone before, then become the starting point for the next stage.

Conclusion

The path of yoga is littered with pitfalls. In the modern era there are two common mistakes which lead to wasted effort and disappointment. The first is to assume yoga is primarily a physical activity and that the desired outcome will be reached by physical practice alone. Often this approach leads people to force the body beyond its limit (no pain, no gain) which regularly leads to injury and setbacks. The second mistake lies in creating a fantasy about where one is in the practice of yoga. Confusion then arises between real and imagined mental states. Meditation as described in the hatha yoga texts requires a firm physical structure to support this process. Many attempt to enter states of meditation without undertaking the necessary physical preparation. The yoga texts repeatedly warn that this is dangerous and can lead to all kinds of problems. It is often likened to trying to enter a cage with a wild animal, not having first taken the steps to become familiar with it and tame it.

It is difficult to know how to proceed on this path as there is little in the yoga texts to guide one from where most people begin nowadays. There are usually physical restrictions and difficulties that need to be addressed as well as mental issues such as poor concentration and stress. It is usually these difficulties that bring a person to yoga in the first place.

This book is primarily for those at such a starting point. It outlines a process where the body, breath and mind are cultivated simultaneously through simple movements. The capacity of the mind to pay attention and respond appropriately grows as the connection between the movements and breathing develops. While working with the different practices, one will become aware of individual strengths and weaknesses. Some will find it easier to squat than to bend forwards or easier to sit cross-legged rather than kneel. For others it will be the opposite. Some people will find coordination and mental concentration easier than others. In the more difficult positions, often one finds as much mental resistance to letting go as in the physical tension or obstruction. Learning to connect with the breath will reduce much of the physical tension and restrictions encountered but this can also present its own challenges. Initially it will demand a deeper mental concentration in ways that may be unfamiliar and sometimes uncomfortable. The deeper, more subtle changes require time and patience. It is a continuous process of opening up sometimes physically, sometimes mentally and sometimes both. The integration of the body and mind that arises goes beyond the sum of the individual parts. One might experience moments when one realises a change

Conclusion

has occurred that appears to have no apparent connection to the activity, or spontaneously become aware of deeper aspects of the practice previously unimagined. These insights will provide deep inspiration and guidance for those who choose this path. The movements or shapes where one has most difficulty often yield the greatest benefits in the long term as they open the door to a hidden potential that lies within. It is only our habitual mind that prevents us from unlocking that potential.

Bibliography

Goraksanātha, Siddha, *Siddhānta Paddhatiḥ - A treatise on the nātha philosophy*, Bhangarwadi, Lonavla India, Lonavla Institute 2005.

Krishnamacharya, T. (author) Desikachar, T.K.V. (translator), *Nathamuni's Yoga Rahasya,* Chennai, India Krishnamacharya Yoga Mandiram 1998.

Shandor Remete, *Shadow Yoga Chaya Yoga - The Principles of Hatha Yoga* Berkeley, California North Atlantic Books 2010.

Sir John Woodroffe, *The Garland of Letters - Studies in the Mantra Śāstra* Ganesh & Co. Madras, India 2011.

Sundaradeva, *Hatha Tattva Kaumudi - A Treatise on Hatha Yoga by Sundaradeva* Bhangarwadi, Lonavla India, Lonavla Institute 2007.

Vasant Lad, *Textbook of Ayurveda - Fundamental Principles* The Ayurvedic Press Albuquerque New Mexico USA 2002.